Felicia Skene

The shadow of the Holy Week

Felicia Skene

The shadow of the Holy Week

ISBN/EAN: 9783742835833

Manufactured in Europe, USA, Canada, Australia, Japa

Cover: Foto ©Lupo / pixelio.de

Manufactured and distributed by brebook publishing software
(www.brebook.com)

Felicia Skene

The shadow of the Holy Week

The

Shadow of the Holy Week.

BY THE AUTHOR OF

"THE DIVINE MASTER."

"He turneth the shadow of death into the morning."

LONDON:

J. MASTERS AND CO., 78, NEW BOND STREET.

1883.

The Shadow of the Holy Week.

Palm Sunday.

THE dawn of a fair spring day has flooded all the eastern land with brilliant sunshine, the calm blue sky is without a cloud throughout its serene expanse, and every hill and valley far and near smiles in the golden light; the soft air echoes with the song of birds and the voices of laughing children, while the crowds that are passing to and fro on their business or their pleasure, seem to have caught on their happy faces all the radiance of the morning. Yes! there is brightness everywhere, save in one spot; over the city of the Great King—Jerusalem—the joy of the whole earth, there lies a strange portentous shadow, unseen to the multitudes who throng its streets or to those who gaze on the Temple buildings from afar, but visible to One Who from all eternity has foreknown the meaning of that mysterious gloom and all that it portends.

It is the shadow of impending Doom; the doom not of death alone, but of every concentrated agony which can be endured by a Victim in Whose awful Being are united the human nature and the Godhead. JESUS has drawn nigh unto Jerusalem. He stands upon the mount of Olives. He looks towards the guilty city, of which it shall be said, in that last Day when the heavens and the earth must flee away before the Face of the Almighty Judge, that there the LORD was crucified. He takes His way along the path that leads to it, in meek and lowly guise ; and while all the world around Him is glad with joy and sunshine, He passes in beneath the shadow that enshrouds it like a funeral pall—*Jesus entered into Jerusalem.*

As it was in the springtide of that momentous year which is linked to all cycles of time, before and since, by the power of an Undying Love, so is it in these latter days, when for us tenanting the earth in our generation, once more the winter has passed and gone, and the singing of birds is heard among the opening flowers ; the gladness and beauty of early spring is around us again and all are rejoicing in the reviving nature, the tread of eager feet tells of the ceaseless search for pleasure or excitement, while mirthful voices echo through the air and the smile of the sunshine is reflected on hopeful faces ; only amid the universal brightness there is now even as there was then, one spot shrouded in mournful darkness, for the eyes that will to behold it. Over the Jerusalem of Passiontide the shadow lies of His remembered Doom, and they who would in true commemoration watch with Him through all His hours of Agony, must turn from the smiling world and its joys, to enter with Him into the precincts of death and pain beneath that veil of ominous gloom.

Let us go that in spirit we may die with Him. JESUS enters into Jerusalem and all the city is moved, saying, "*Who is this ?*" At the entrance of Holy Week we answer, "He is our life,"— even as, on the threshold of the world beyond the grave, we hope to say, "He is our Life Eternal."

Within the limit of these seven days we may
see concentrated, the whole mystery of that Redemption of the human race, which stretches
from everlasting to everlasting in the changeless
purpose of the Infinite GOD. In the progress
of JESUS from the triumphant palm-strewn way,
to the Sepulchre sealed in darkness and silence
beneath the great stone, there is a close analogy
with every stage of mortal existence, and we
shall find that the manner of His being from
hour to hour, touches all forms of possible dis-
cipline by which we may be moulded into His
Likeness, and drawn into union with the Living
GOD.

For us, the Incarnation, the Passion, and the
Sacrifice all proclaim the same Truth, that the
intense desire of happiness, the inappeasable
craving for an unknown good, which is coexistent
with our very consciousness, can have its satis-
faction only in Him, Who is the manifest Love
of GOD, since it is but the inevitable search for
the one object of our being, the demand, uncom-
prehended by ourselves, of our GOD-created
spirits for that LORD of Life Who has made us
for Himself.

Once it was said unto JESUS, "*All men seek*

Thee," and in these words was revealed the secret which lies at the heart of all humanity. It is JESUS Whom every living soul is seeking ; it is the dumb unconscious supplication of their very nature, for Him Who is the Bliss, the Life, the Eternity, that alone can fill their deathless spirits, which speaks in all the restlessness, the futile struggling in disappointment and despair, that load this world with a thousand forms of anguish.

If we enter with Him now beneath the shadow of the Holy Week, we shall learn in each one of its ever darkening hours, not only, how truly it is for JESUS that unknowingly we seek from the first moment of earthly existence to the last, but after what manner also, the probation of every stage of mortal life is fashioned in union with that Sacrifice of Suffering, whereby alone He has placed within our reach the beatitude of His Eternal Love.

The very first accents of the Divine Voice, which we hear as we pass with Him into the shrouded city of the Passion, proclaim this the central Truth of our whole being.

" *If thou hadst known, even thou, in this thy day, the things that belong unto thy peace,*"—

and—*Jesus wept!*—Not only for Jerusalem, nor
for all the myriads living on the earth that day,
but for every individual soul who has ever
entered on probation here, and to whom those
words have been spoken in vain, so that they
have reached the bourne of troubled tortured
life without having realized that He, and He
alone, is our Peace. He wept in that hour for
the suffering He knew that each one through
all succeeding ages should endure, whoever
sought for happiness or rest apart from Him.
Shall not the thought of those tears fall like
heavenly dew upon the aching hearts, that vainly
have beat so high for the delusive hopes of earth,
telling us that although we have turned aside
deceived, from Him our only good, yet can His
Divine compassion reach us still, and He Who
wept for us is ready even now to wipe away all
our tears ?

If thou hadst known—even thou—thy Peace.

Let us enter on the seven awful days, bearing
those words within our hearts as the solution of
the problems of life for us and for all mankind.
To each separate human being there comes at
some period of their lives, the time of their
visitation which is known only to their own souls

and to their GOD, but the recurrence of this Holy Week is also in its measure a time of visitation, of which the responsibility will surely rest upon us all for weal or for woe.

It is the dawn of the first Palm Sunday, and we see in it the type of the morning of existence. Whether those springtide years are with us still, or looking back we see them from the toilsome paths of later life, the lesson taught us is the same. "*Behold, thy King cometh,*" and they say unto Him, "*Hosanna in the highest. Blessed is He that cometh in the Name of the Lord.*"

Their adoration for the moment is sincere, yet these are they who later in the march of time shall cry out, " Crucify Him, crucify Him, we have no king but Cæsar !" They deceived themselves, they believed that they loved Him, that they desired to have Him for their only King, but when to own Him meant peril and pain, they cast Him out to die, and gave to the earthly monarch their allegiance and their truth.

Has it not been even so with ourselves ? We were called by the name of CHRIST in our early youth, and believed that we were surely His in loyalty and faith. We adored Him as our King, and offered Him the fragile flowers we plucked upon the sunlit paths wherein we were content to follow Him, but when the royal march with waving palms and songs exultant led into the Dolorous Way, when the shadow closed around Him, when the sunshine of joy and the flowers of life were all left far behind Him, when He entered into the temple of our spirits and demanded that He should reign there as our only King and GOD,—did we not shrink from the terrible sentence uttered at that very temple door, "*He that loveth his life shall lose it, and he that hateth his life in this world shall keep it unto life eternal.*"

Did we not love the fair expanse of years which seemed to stretch out before us, bright with the golden promise of imagined joys, the royal gifts which the Cæsar of this world could bestow, to whom our hearts went out in secret homage, while outwardly we seemed to worship CHRIST the LORD? Not only, perhaps, in youth, but even to this day may it not have been so with us? If in this our hearts condemn us, then may we feel indeed that Holy Week has brought to us the time of our visitation, for the

special warning of Palm Sunday bids us look
to it, lest unknowingly we have deceived ourselves with a fair show of outward homage to
the Crucified, while in our secret heart we
adored the world-power who could gild for us
the fleeting days of earthly life. Γνῶθι σεαυτὸν,
know thyself, judge thyself this day, that the
Sacred Victim Who would draw thee after Him
now into the shadow of His Passion, judge thee
not hereafter as a self-deceiver, in the piercing
light of the Great White Throne.

This is the lesson of the first of the seven
holy days, but each one is marked by a special
consolation for those who are true to their Redeemer, no less than by a definite warning to
all who may be false to Him in heart,—and
now from the rebuke we turn to the blessing.

How far soever we have sought to satisfy with
the fair false joys of earth that longing for happiness which is in truth but the thirst of our
souls for the living GOD, in such measure we
have most surely suffered as the sole result of
our vain endeavours, and shall suffer haply to
the end ; but for all the pain and bitter disappointment we thus have gathered to ourselves,
there is in this day of Palms a gift of tender

healing, since He in these first hours of Holy Week takes on Himself an anguish similar in kind, differing only in its sinlessness, so that the comfort wherewith He and He alone can comfort us is given in perfect sympathy. Does not all seem to promise joy and brightness for Him that day when the eager voices cry, "*Hosanna*," and hail Him as their Beloved, their King for Whom no flowers can be too fair, no honour done too great ? and yet He knew even then how their love would turn to hatred, their welcome to rejection; how they would nail unto the cruel Cross the Feet for which they made the way soft with their very garments, and flood His last hours with bitterness Whom they had called blessed in His coming. Therefore does He enter this day with full comprehension into the secret bitterness that fills our hearts when all that seemed most fair, most true, most dear, turns in our grasp to ashes, and the sympathy of JESUS, unlike the barren compassions of this world, has power to replace the pain which draws it forth with an undying joy ; for He knows that we suffer only because we sought our happiness apart from our one essential Bliss, and even with tears He offers Himself to fill our souls with rapture. "*If thou hadst known, even thou, thy Peace.*"

Let us not pass, then, from the day of Palms without having taken into our lives the warning to know ourselves, to prove whether we are His in sincerity and truth and possess Him in unspeakable blessedness as our only and eternal Peace.

And now the first day of the Holy Week is over, "*Jesus departed and hid Himself.*"

There can be no certainty where the LORD spent that first night of His Passion, for while some old writers have supposed that He went to Bethany, there are others, nearer to that awful time, who believed that He resorted to no house of friends, but that each night of the five which preceded the final sacrifice, was passed by Him within that Garden of Gethsemane where He was at the last to receive from His FATHER'S Hands the cup of agony.[1]

---

[1] It is evident that Judas knew where to find his Master when he came to deliver Him up to His enemies, and this was believed in earlier times to give a strong proof that all the nights of Holy Week were spent by the LORD on the Mount of Olives.

Monday in Holy Week.

HE sun has risen again, still fair in its springtide dawn, but the Shadow deepens on the second day of the mournful seven. Gone is all semblance even of triumph and of welcome, none hail the Victim now as King or call Him blessed, no triumphal palms are borne before Him or garments spread beneath His weary Feet as in a royal progress. Slowly He returns, spent with vigil and fasting, from His mysterious solitude to the city of His doom, and none are by His side save the few that only for a little time as yet, are faithful to their dying LORD. But we who have entered into the Shadow of the Holy Week are with Him there, and we stand on the wayside path as He draws near. He has seen that which afar off seems a fair and fruitful tree, making a pleasant show with its bright green leaves, and rearing its stately head to heaven as if eager to catch the light and dew which fall from thence. Surely with such rich and fertile seeming it is ready to minister to Him with all its growth, with all its capabilities? He comes hungering to find fruit thereon,—but there is none.

He by Whom all things were made had breathed into it the breath of life, which enabled it to bring forth all those waving branches with their weight of leaves,—but beneath that outward appearance of homage to its Creator all is hollow and barren. Not there shall His hunger for the offerings of living love be stayed,—not there shall He see the travail of His soul and be satisfied. This day in our ear sounds again the mournful sentence, "*Let no fruit grow on thee henceforward for ever.*" Well may we shudder as we hear it, for it may be that in the fair deceptive tree with its goodly show of specious beauty we see the type of our own selves, in the golden prime of life when the careless days of youth are past, and the world allures us with its most subtle charm through the praise and goodwill of our fellow-men. Has not the secret desire to win their admiration and their love been the true motive power that has decked our lives with fairest deeds and robed us in an external garb of all that is most lovely and of good report? May not the very homage and devotion offered to our only LORD have been made sweet to us by the human approbation and applause it has won us in this lower world? Pleasant to the eye has our daily existence seemed perhaps, rich in acts of charity and religious fervour, but shall the LORD find beneath the fruits of the Spirit which He seeks?

Love—pure and unreserved for Himself alone.

Joy—sought and found in communion with Him only.

Peace—such as apart from Him can have no existence.

Longsuffering—practised in likeness of Him Who forgave His murderers.

Gentleness—learned from Him Who when He was reviled, reviled not again.

Goodness—inspired by union with Him Who alone is good.

Faith—by secret knowledge of Him in Whom unseen His own believe.

Meekness—won at His Feet Who trod the lowest paths for our poor sake.

Temperance—because in Him to do our FA-
THER'S will is all we ask or seek.

Has He found these fruits of a vital union
with Himself when He came to us hungering
for proofs of our sure eternal blessedness? or
is it so with us, despite our fair show in the flesh,
that He may justly say even now, " *Behold, I
come seeking fruit on this fig-tree, and find
none . . . . cut it down, why cumbereth it the
ground ?*"

If our unreal service has hitherto provoked
this dreadful sentence, yet in the merciful per-
mission to pass once more beneath the Shadow
of this Holy Week we hear the voice of Divine
Compassion saying, " *I will let it alone this
year also, and dig about it . . . and if it bear
fruit, well,—if not, after that shall it be cut
down.*" Blessed indeed is the renewed gift of
these days of our visitation, for is there one
amongst us who has not at some time of in-
sidious temptation loved the praise of men,
more than the acceptance of a true service by
Him Whose unprofitable servants we, at the
best, must ever be ? Yet a sterner warning
against human respect and unreality is given
now as we follow Him within the gates of the

temple to which He passes on, the consecrated
House of GOD.   There we behold Him the
meek and patient LORD, suddenly manifesting
Himself awful and severe in His righteous in-
dignation, as He casts out all earthly treasures
from the sacred place which the Eternal FA-
THER had chosen as the habitation of His Spirit.
Surely heinous indeed must have been the sin
which provoked the *wrath of the Lamb*.   He
Who under cruelest persecution does not strive
or cry, Who as a sheep before her shearers is
dumb in presence of His murderers, yet now
with relentless sternness denounces those who
have made that house of prayer a den of thieves.
It is our Judge Who speaks. He looks now into
our spirit, the temple of the HOLY GHOST which
we should have held for Him, immaculate, His
dwelling-place undefiled, unshared, whence the
pure offering should have risen up continually
of a faithful service—an entire surrender of the
whole being unto Him our only LORD and Love.
What if like that temple of old He sees in the
sanctuary of our souls but a den of thieves, of
earthly desires and hopes which have stolen
away from Him our best affections?—what am-
bitions and vanities, what love of the world and

of self,—what secret sins and unchastened long-
ings may have robbed Him of all the true devotion of our hearts ! If it be so, shall we not be-
seech Him this day to cast out from the temple
of our spirit all things, be they what they may,
which mar the exclusive supremacy of His reign
within us ? Dear and precious may be to us the
treasures which we have suffered to invade His
chosen shrine,—so dear that for their continu-
ance in our possession, rather than for a closer
union with Himself, may have ever arisen the
petitions that gave it the semblance of a house
of prayer, and bitter may be to us the anguish
of their rending away from our clinging hold.
Yet even with the sharpest scourge of pain let
us call on Him to drive them from us. Then
shall the special consolation of this second day
be ours,—for it is to the soul that flings away
all its earthly idols to give itself to Him alone
that He utters the blessed words, "*I will not
leave you comfortless, I will come to you.*"
JESUS Whom we and all men for ever seek un-
consciously, will come to us and make His
abode within the cleansed sanctuary of our
spirit, to be our Life and Love, our everlasting
joy.

C

Upon that very day when He thus manifested His claim to the unreserved allegiance of the human race He knew that His enemies were taking counsel to kill Him,—and as it was then so is it now.   While those who do desire, however feebly, to follow Him in life and death are beseeching Him beneath the shadow of His Passion to make their spirits meet for His abode, outside in the garish sunlight of the world men are conspiring to kill Him in the souls of His people, and to brand with the infamy of falsehood His faith and Name.   Surely of them as of us that Divine One thought in His undying pity, when the evening being now come He departed without the city to the solitude where through all these prophetic nights, He gazed into the depths of that anguish of sacrifice which could alone redeem the world's iniquity.

Tuesday in Holy Week.

THE shadow deepens yet more on the third of the mournful Passion days. The LORD returns from His lonely watch, to speak for the last time within His desecrated Temple to the people who hated Him, and for whom He was about to die; and as He journeys towards the city the first sight that meets His sorrowful gaze is the fig-tree withered away. It is the emblem of His dread prerogative of justice and of punishment. He Whose very Being is essential Love, Who yearns to gather all that have ever drawn the breath of human life into His compassionate arms, is yet of purer eyes than to behold iniquity, and even from His tender lips must fall the awful sentence, " *Depart, ye cursed.*"

Dark lies the shadow then upon the bare dis-

torted branches of the withered tree, type of the
judgment to come, and thence He passes on to
utter His final warnings within the sacred walls
where never again shall His Divine Voice be
heard in human accents.

Even as the LORD was visibly present then
within His chosen temple, so is He present now
within His Church on earth, and as then He
spoke, so does He speak to us now in the commemoration of this sacred week.—With the eight
Beatitudes His ministry on earth began,—by
those heavenly words of blessing breathed as
it were from the very heart of the love of GOD,
He ushered in the teaching of the gospel of
peace ; but now with the shadow round Him
of that voluntary Death, in which so many for
whom it was consummated would fail to see
their only life, He closes His public testimony,
by pronouncing the eight awful woes on all self-
seeking and hypocrisy.

Woe unto us if by an example of worldliness
or an unworthy use of the gift of influence, we
hinder the efforts of those who are aiming at
a height we would not have them reach, because we have not sought ourselves to attain
unto it.

Woe unto us if we have sought the accomplishment of our own desires at the expense of others and have loved ourselves more even than GOD'S own poor, while unto their FATHER and ours we cease not to turn in unfelt prayers.

Woe unto us if we seek to proselytize to our narrow views, those who hold the Truth in ways distasteful to our vanity or our party spirit,— if we will not have them live severely while we dwell in luxury, or turn from a world that is dear unto ourselves, or seek to serve their GOD save at our bidding and in our measure, because we would have them careless and frivolous even as we are.

Woe unto us if we exalt external forms of religion above the secret heart-service of Him Whose indwelling Presence in our souls, alone gives them value or reality.

Woe unto us if we have made our Christianity to consist in trifling observances, and clung with vehemence and angry defiance to matters of detail, while we neglect utterly the true worship of GOD in mercy, judgment, and faith.

Woe unto us if while we use all Sacramental ordinances for the cleansing of our souls in the sight of GOD and man, we yet fail to purge them inwardly of the evil thoughts and passions that defile them in secret.

Woe unto us if we appear to be white and fair in all the beauty of holiness, while by a subtle hypocrisy, scarce known to ourselves, we are concealing many a hidden sin that lies corrupting within us.

Woe unto us if while we adorn the House of GOD and show all reverence to the memory of His departed saints, we yet persecute those of His living people who differ from us, or despise and neglect them because they are humble and of low estate.

Thus it was that throughout the whole of that last day of the LORD'S ministry on earth, the burden of His teaching was ever against that hidden deep-rooted self-love which fatally destroys the Love of GOD within us, however specious an appearance of it we may wear even in our own eyes.

When the eight Woes had been pronounced, falling dread and solemn on the air as the strokes of a funeral bell sounding the knell of criminals approaching to their doom, then did the LORD begin to speak to His people in parables. Each one while it foreshadowed His own swift coming death for our redemption, told also how we and many in the generations yet to come would crucify Him anew, by giving to the world and to our chosen idols the love and fealty He bought to be His own at the cost of His priceless Sacrifice. *"This is the Heir, come, let us kill Him, and the inheritance shall be ours."*

We long to enjoy the sweets of life rather than to labour in His vineyard through heat and cold, in pain and thirst and hunger,—and it may be that we have acted as though we had said, "Let us kill Him in our hearts, that the inheritance of this fair world and all its joys may yet be ours."

"Then said He to His servants, The marriage is ready." We have seen how He has spread a table for us in the wilderness of this world, with the Eucharistic Feast whereby we are bound to Him in the power of that resurrection life which shall merge into eternal union, when we drink with Him of the new chalice at the marriage supper of the Lamb; but have we come to the foretaste, at His earthly altar, of the hour when He shall raise us up from the dead, without having probed the secret depths of our

spirits, only perhaps to find them yet so filled with human hopes and desires that there is no room for Him to take up His abode within us in sacramental fulness?

"*Then shall the kingdom of Heaven be likened unto ten virgins, which took their lamps, and went forth to meet the Bridegroom.*"

We have ostensibly been going forth to meet Him from that first hour when His name was given us in the baptismal waters, and through all the years that we have lived since then, we have borne our lamps with their flickering uncertain light before the world's eyes, but how shall it be with us when the midnight cry is heard of His dear coming? Did not the LORD say centuries before He came to us on earth, that He would only accept the offering of "*oil for the light and for sweet incense,*" which is given willingly *with the heart?* and if ours has been but a scanty grudging supply, surely the oil will fail and the Light fade out in our lamp before the brightness of His unveiled Presence.

"*A certain nobleman . . . . called his ten servants, and delivered them ten pounds, and said unto them, Occupy till I come.*"

So too of the gifts which He entrusted to us

each one according to our several ability, that we should use them for the increase of His kingdom upon earth, and the winning of many helpless souls to enter with us into His eternal joy. What if we have held aloof from His erring wanderers, the ignorant, the poor, the sinful, wrapt in our own pride and selfishness,— preserving His gifts intact, but all unfruitful, so that when the hour comes to render them back we can but come before Him alone with empty hands and say, "*There Thou hast that is Thine.*"

Finally, the teaching of that sad day culminates in the most awful words that ever sounded from the Divine lips on earth,—the words truly in which are summed up all promise of undying joy, all warning of unutterable pain : the beatitudes of His first utterances contending again with the woes of His last, in the ineffable summons, "*Come, ye blessed,*" and the dreadful sentence, "*Depart, ye cursed.*"

"*When Jesus had finished all these sayings, He went out of the temple.*" And well may we believe that the only faint gleam of light which relieved the dark shadow of that day for Him, was in the crystal purity of that clear shining love which enabled the poor widow to offer to her GOD not of her slender substance only, but all that she had, "*even all her living.*"

If the warning of this day against self-seeking in its most subtle forms cuts deep into our very heart, striking at the root of our most hidden desires, yet is there a consolation waiting on our acceptance of that searching pain, which transcends in its unspeakable sweetness, far as the heavens above the earth, the worst agony we can endure,—for when the soul is emptied of self, then, and then alone, will CHRIST come to abide within it in fulness of possession, and the bitter pangs of renunciation give place to rapturous peace, when we hear stealing on our consciousness the words that seem to echo from the very Throne of GOD, "*Lo, I am with you always.*"

Wednesday in Holy Week.

DEEPER than at any time, except on the awful hours of sacrifice, the Shadow of the Holy Week falls on the fourth morning, for it is the day of the betrayal, of darkest treachery.

Weak, erring, sinful as we are, we yet are striving to follow the LORD in the mournful path of His Passion. We have loved Him, we do love Him feebly, imperfectly, no doubt, yet still in such measure that it seems to us impossible we can need any warning against the hideous crime which makes this day more accursed than any other that has ever been branded by the enmity of man to GOD. Yet He Who said of His very torturers, when with loud sounding strokes they drove the cruel nails into His Hands and Feet, "*they know not what they do,*" could well foresee far reaching to the

end of time the manifold unfaithfulness whereby
He yet should be daily, hourly betrayed in
hidden acts by those who believe themselves to
be indeed His own.

Most sorrowful of all the Passion days surely
was this to Him, bitterer, sadder even than the
terrible death day, for into the consummation
of the Cross there entered the blessed foreknowledge of the salvation which it purchased
for all that would receive it of the erring human
race, but there is not so much as a thought of
comfort to relieve the blackness of treachery
which stamps with infamy the pitiless day of
the betrayal. Well might it be said of it, "*Let
that day be darkness; let not God regard it from
above, neither let the light shine upon it.*"
Calmly, gently, the LORD had announced its
coming to His disciples without a word of reproach, or of the bitter anguish it would bring
to Him Whose very Being was perfect love.
He had closed His public teaching upon earth
with the one word "*Watch*," the solemn em-
phatic word that reverberates through all the
vanished centuries on every living soul with its
concentrated warning. Then without comment
He divulged the secret act of Judas.

"And it came to pass when Jesus had finished all these sayings, He said unto His disciples, Ye know that after two days is the feast of the Passover, and the Son of Man is betrayed,—and at night He went out and abode in the mount that is called the mount of Olives."

"He abode in the mount." No other record is given of the period which elapsed between His last farewell to the glorious temple, so soon like the Sacred Body of which it was the type, to be delivered into the hands of ruthless men, and that divine hour when He was to celebrate the Holy Mysteries for the first time in the upper room. It seems plain, therefore, that throughout the veiled day of His betrayal, when no sign of His Presence on earth is given to us in His Holy Word, He abode in the mount, bearing on His Heart before the Just Eternal GOD the multitudes that should betray Him. Not for Judas only did the Son of Man agonize beneath the Shadow of His Passion during the long hours when He knew that the archtraitor was taking counsel with His enemies against the Anointed of the LORD, goaded on by the unseen accuser of the brethren, although to Him Who loves each individual soul as if none other

existed in the universe, the hideous treachery
of that one false follower must in truth have
pierced His divine heart with an intolerable
pain.

"*It is not an open enemy that hath done Me
this dishonour, for then I could have borne it,
but it was even thou My companion, Mine own
familiar friend.*"

Borne by the sighing wind to the murmuring
trees around Him, He must in His omniscience
have heard the voice that had so often spoken
to Him in words of love and reverence now
whispering to His foes, "*What will ye give me,
and I will deliver Him unto you?*"

He had willed so fully to assume our human
nature, that He might be able to share in every
sinless pang which we can feel, and thus the
cruel defection of a trusted friend must have
brought such a bitterness of pain as some
amongst us may have known perhaps only too
well, while far beyond our comprehension must
have been the awful suffering wrought on the
SON of GOD by His foreknowledge of the
traitor's doom. All this, we dare not doubt,—
this anguish in its twofold form, was multiplied
that day in the fathomless spirit of the LORD of

all, by every thought, and word, and deed of unfaithfulness whereby He knew He should ever be betrayed in the ages yet to come.

As we watch by Him there beneath the ever-deepening shadow, does not our awakened conscience sting us with keenest pang as it reveals to us the many occasions when by a subtle scarce conscious treachery we may have ourselves betrayed Him? The thirty pieces of silver which tempted the traitor to his hateful crime have appeared to us in guise of all these fair allurements of the world which cannot be enjoyed consistently with unreserved devotion to the Crucified LORD. Whenever our own pleasure or the claims of our earthly affections have stood between us and our Redeemer, we have betrayed Him, but these are forms of treachery which are easily detected ; there are others of a far more specious nature whereby we may too surely have done so more completely.

In these days when pride of intellect, of scientific progress, and of freedom have all alike arrayed themselves against the LORD and His written Word, are we not often tempted to shrink from drawing down contempt upon ourselves by upholding openly the old faiths which so called enlightenment has trampled under foot? It is easy to say to ourselves that we are too weak to argue with stronger minds, that it is better to be silent even when our Master is traduced, than to give feeble and uncertain support to His holy truth; but let us examine our souls in sight of Him Whose mournful eyes in these sad hours looked down the vista of the future to its uttermost limit, and noted every shade of unfaithfulness which should mar the union of His people with Himself, and we shall surely detect that not humility but human respect held us back from speaking boldly in the name of CHRIST whenever His Faith has in any way been assailed in our presence. May we not also find too probably that we have tacitly connived at forms of error whether in doctrine or practice, under the spurious guise of a charity that seeks to veil the faults of others? Then, indeed, do we betray the Son of Man with a kiss, as also when we use our influence as one of His professed followers for any selfish purpose of our own.

In other and in simpler ways it may be that we betray Him daily. We are vowed to His unflinching service by His Sacraments and our own will, and wheresoever we have failed in perseverance or in sternest duty, we may in our measure have betrayed Him every hour. Truly the dread that in these and many other ways we may be self-deceiving traitors to our beloved LORD, causes the shadow of this day to lie with a dense and heavy gloom upon our spirits. Yet is the consolation which the Divine One offers to us all, if only we faint and fail not, through this our little day of earthly life, more dear, more entrancing in its promises than human thought can ever compass, since far beyond the confines of the grave that once enclosed Him, far above the mighty stone which the angels rolled away from His deserted tomb, from out the Beatific Vision of the Resurrection Life, the Voice of Him Who was dead and is alive sounds like the fall of living waters in the glorious words, " *Be thou faithful unto death, and I will give thee a crown of life.*"

Maundy Thursday.

AND now the day of love has dawned, so perfectly the day consecrated to the Divine Eternal Charity by its special teaching, and by the Institution of the Sacrament of love, that it might almost seem to us as if no Shadow could dim the Heavenly aspect of those hours, wherein the LORD showed forth by words and deeds ineffable His undying tenderness for His followers, and for all who should in the ages to come, believe on Him through their word.

"*Having loved His own which were in the world, He loved them to the end.*"

What pain, what grief or earthly trial could outlive these words, if indeed we had in no way forfeited our claim to hold them in everlasting possession as our inalienable inheritance ?   But fair and gracious as is the Light, which Love would fain have shed on this fifth Passion day, it is obscured and well nigh blotted out by the deep appalling shadow that steals up from the dark garden of the Agony, and teaches us that this manifestation of Infinite Love could only be given to us through the ministry of infinite pain.

" *The Master saith, My time is at hand.*"

The earlier hours of this day, thè last on which He should see the sun go down in His earthly life, are veiled in the same mystery as that which shrouded Him throughout the day of His betrayal from all human knowledge ; doubtless because they were spent in secret communion with the FATHER ; but, "*when the even was come He entered into the large upper room with His disciples,*" and thither let us follow Him beneath the shadow of the most blessed, and yet most awful night that ever fell upon the world of His creation.

Of all that took place between the entrance of the LORD into the guest-chamber, and His departure from Gethsemane, as the willing captive of the foes who had been stricken to the ground by the Majesty of His Presence, it were too presumptuous even to touch in this the faintest, feeblest expression of the thoughts that must be with us on this momentous night. We dare only to fall down with silent adoration before the unsearchable riches of the Divine Eucharist, by which, from that hour every living soul that wills to be redeemed of CHRIST, may be linked to Him in everlasting union. Is it not enough to show us all, what the Sacrament of His Body and Blood must be to our salvation, that He who never so much as breathed a wish for Himself, should now with almost passionate force proclaim, how with desire had He desired to eat *this* Passover before He suffered, that through the Divine Feast into which it was merged, the destroying angel, in the last dread day might see His Blood sprinkled on the souls of His people, and pass them by when he goes forth to slay His enemies before Him.

So too, we leave untouched that wondrous sacramental act, whereby our Master showed that He, to Whom has been given power over all flesh, that He might give them eternal life, can yet only enable us to have part in Him by washing us in His own Blood ; not once alone in the washing of regeneration, but daily, hourly, so that the dust of this corrupting world which clings to our feet as we tread its tortuous ways, may be ever and ever cleansed away. In like manner inspired by His Divine example, He bids us prove that we have truly part in Him, by serving Him humbly and thankfully in the persons of His poorer brethren on earth. While we thus shrink however from dwelling on the great acts of this solemn night, there are some of the sacred words spoken then, when He delivered to the world that which may be called the Gospel of the Agony, that are to us in this rebellious age, so especially the words of Eternal life, that they seem to stand out from all surrounding gloom as though written in letters of light, and to them we gladly turn. The first of those Divine utterances which echo with undying power from that upper room upon our listening spirits, is that which stamps this day with the dazzling yet terrible effulgence of His Love and its claim to our obedience in the Church His Body.

"*A new commandment give I unto you—that ye love one another as I have loved you.*"

As He has loved us! *we* are to love one

another as He has loved us! we with our self-seeking desires, our idolatrous hearts, our violent passions, our strong antipathies, we are to love as He loved,—the Incarnate GOD, Who in ceaseless suffering laid down not only His life for His friends, but also, all the glory that He had with the Eternal FATHER before the worlds were.

How awful a command! high as the Heavens in its exalted comprehensiveness, yet not impossible even for us when joined in Sacramental union with Him our LORD, for before He uttered that commandment He instituted the Sacred mysteries, whereby we can so be sharers in His own Divine nature as to make it possible for us to obey it.

He proclaims the unearthly mandate which gives its name to the fifth Passion day, He creates the Sacrament of essential union with Himself whereby alone it may be kept, and then, as if in His unutterable mercy to lure us to its fulfilment by the most powerful motive, which could sway the souls of His people, He says unto us,

"*If ye love Me keep My commandments,*"—and this last above all, the last before He suffered.

So far then as we have not loved one another,

even as He has loved us, we have proved that
we have not loved Him, the dying LORD about
to offer Himself in torments inconceivable, a
Sacrifice for us! The obligation laid upon us
therefore by the very nature of this day, is the
deliberate searching scrutiny of our hearts and
lives, to drag out of their inmost depths, every
evidence of the extent to which we have failed
to love our brethren as CHRIST has loved us.
What a terrible light will that probing of conscience fling upon our own share, in causing the
mysterious agony, which bowed the LORD of
Heaven to the very earth that night, beneath
the weight of all the world's iniquity! Have
we ever so much as given Him any real proof
that we love Him, by the perfect keeping of
this new, this last commandment? if no other
sin of ours were laid upon Him, save those
which we have heaped together by its nonfulfil-
ment, we have no need to wonder at the great
drops of Blood wrung from Him by His untold
anguish.

Truly the warning of this day against un-
charitableness in all the manifold meanings of
the term, is sharper than a two-edged sword
when it pierces into our self-deceiving hearts,

and opens up to us the depths of our failure to
love the brethren and in them the Elder Brother
of the family of man.

Yet this the saddest evening that ever cast its
shadow on all time, brings to us through the
words spoken by the dying SAVIOUR, consolations more priceless in their value to our fainting struggling souls than any that can come to
us on brightest festivals.

We are groping here amid the unsolved problems of this bewildering world, met at every
turn by the inexplicable mystery of evil, by the
permitted suffering of the innocent and helpless,
by the inscrutable conditions of our own being,
while all around us, sound the mocking voices
of this age of so called progress, telling us that
our faith is false, our hopes are vain, that CHRIST
is not risen from the dead, and we are of all men
most miserable : and surely the whole mental
torture of this chaos of doubt and difficulty was
foreseen by Him, when, having proclaimed His
Deity by bidding us believe in Him even as we
believe in GOD, and told us that He was about
to prepare a place where we, in unchanged iden-
tity, should live for ever in deathless realms,
He turned and gave to all future generations the

calm assurance, "*If it were not so I would have told you.*"

He, the living Truth, would not have deceived us. He would not have left us one moment in a false hope, Who gave Himself to save us from despair. If He were not GOD, Incarnate for our sakes, He would have told us. If there were no life beyond the grave, no future of immortality, no place for any of the human race in the eternal Mansions of His FATHER, He would have told us. He did not endure an earthly existence of toil and humiliation, and a voluntary death of torture, to mock with baseless fables, those for whom He died. If for us there awaited only annihilation in the dust of mortal corruption He would have told us. In His infinite compassion and tenderness He bids us not doubt Him, though all the world conspire to blot out His Name from the universe of His creation, for He would have told us if He had not Himself been that Eternal Life which He promised to us in the face of His Own Death.

"*Because I live, ye shall live also.*" Then— then when that everlasting day has dawned, we shall know that He is in the FATHER, and we in Him. This strong consolation wherein we may

take refuge, is not however the only one afforded
to us on that evening. As if still looking forward
to the blasts of atheism and false philosophy that
should in future ages sweep over this insensate
world, the LORD gave us a promise of internal
evidence which no outward argument or proof
can so much as touch in any sense, for He de-
clares to all who strive to keep His commandments, that He will manifest Himself to them.

"*He that hath My commandments, and keep-
eth them, he it is that loveth Me, and I will love
him, and will manifest Myself to him.*"

They shall see and know Him in their inmost
consciousness in such a wondrous certainty of
present intercourse, that the negations of science
or agnosticism must fall powerless on the spirit
wherein He dwells, like the mad waves beating
in vain round an impregnable rock.

Thus it is, that the secret of the LORD is with
them that fear Him, and that with no vain boast
they can affirm to sceptics and cavillers, that
they *know* Him in Whom they have believed,
and thus too is the ineffable promise of that
evening of the agony fulfilled—

"*Ye shall know that I am in My Father, and
ye in Me, and I in you.*"

Nor is this all; it would seem as if in these last hours when JESUS still submitted to the conditions of our mortal nature, He had gauged all the sources of pain or fear which might assail us when we too should face the mystery of death. Even when a sure knowledge of the LORD leaves us no power to doubt that there is an eternal life beyond it, we cannot escape a haunting dread of the unknown conditions of that mysterious future state. The spirit quails before the thought of plunging alone into an unseen immensity, like a fluttering leaf flung out upon the mighty blast, and whirled away through darkness none know whither; and was it not to meet those very terrors that the Dying Voice of the Divine One spoke those words of unutterable blessedness and peace, when He declared, He would come to receive us to Himself—

"That where I am, there ye may be also?"

He willed not to reveal to us in any degree the nature of our being in that further life, but enough—enough beyond all power of language, to express its depths of consolation, is the certainty bequeathed to us in His hour of agony, that howsoever, wheresoever we are, *we shall be with Him.* It is His Will, what room can there ever be again for doubt or trembling in face of death?

"*Father, I will that those whom Thou hast given Me, be with Me where I am.*"

These were among the words spoken by the LORD, when having lifted up His Eyes to Heaven, He entered into that last communion with the Eternal FATHER, of which the awful sanctity seems profaned by any approach in human language, therefore we dare not touch any further on what has been vouchsafed to our knowledge of that supreme hour ; only let us say, "May GOD be praised for ever," that He has allowed the record of these unearthly utterances to remain with us, for the Divinity of the God-head is so stamped upon them, that they alone have had power to smite with irresistible con-viction, souls that else had remained for ever lost in lowest depths of unbelief. Yet although we may not speak of that wondrous Intercession, let us remember, whatever be our trials, our temp-tations, our struggles, our failures, our almost despair, that He prayed then for us, for us poor fainting sinners that should believe on Him through His written Evangel.

And now the rayless shadow of that last Pas-

sion evening so deepens around the Sacred
Victim, that we seem unable to dwell any longer
on these heavenly consolations, for Judas has
gone out to do that which he had to do quickly,
and—"*it was night!*" words of terrible significance!

It was night indeed, profound, unfathomable,
for the traitor and for all who to the end of
time depart in any sense from the Light of the
world; and it was night for Him, the Lamb of
GOD, Whom all creation shall behold hereafter
as the sole Light of Eternity, when "*He went
forth over the brook Cedron, where was a garden into the which He entered.*"

Gethsemane! how can we venture to rest the
eyes of mental vision on that mysterious scene
when in superhuman agony the LORD of all
wrestled with Eternal Justice for the redemption
of the human race?

"*My soul is exceeding sorrowful, even unto
death.*" Not the hosts of heaven who watched
in silence there around their King, thus made a
spectacle to angels and to men, nor any who
have ever lived, could sound the depths of suffering expressed in these gentle, pathetic words,
for on that Innocent Head the Almighty Hand

has bound the sins of all humanity, and laid Him prostrate beneath their weight on the dust of this defiled earth, while the Divine Heart breaks under the awful sense of the FATHER'S wrath for all the transgressions of the guilty race whom He, the only Sinless, represented there.

"*Thy rebuke hath broken My Heart.*"

It is not for us to dwell in open words on a theme so sacred, thankful only may we be if we are permitted in this Holy Week to lie under the Shadow of dark Gethsemane in mute abasement, and make that dread vigil a stern preparation for the hour of our own death, since then for the first time were heard the accents of that sad reproach, which must re-echo again on the soul of every one departing from an existence which has not been truly given to GOD.

"*Could ye not watch with Me one hour?*" This little hour of life! how shall we bear it fainting in dissolution, if through all our years of strength and power we have left Him unheeded in His anguish for our sins, and taken our pleasure in self-willed ease or cold indifference?

"*Sleep on now,*" the sleep of death, till we see Him coming with clouds to judge the world.

It was night, night black with a darkness that may be felt, for the traitor has come and given to the Master, Who was about to die for him, the kiss, which represents all the evil that ever has been done in the name of CHRIST, all human passions indulged under a profession of religion, all unreal, hollow service simulating the perfect way of life.

" Friend, wherefore art thou come ?"

The Divine LORD called Judas still by that dear title, hoping, perhaps, for the traitor's own sake to rouse some lingering spark of affection in his heart ; but we know how Judas delivered Him to His murderers, and bade them hold Him fast.

" Ye are My friends," He had said to His disciples with yet deeper, tenderer meaning : His friends, His own whom He had loved and did love even to the end, and now in His hour of utmost peril, of agony, of certain swift-coming death—

" They all forsook Him and fled."

In the entire desolation of that moment there fell upon Him Who has borne our griefs and carried our sorrows, a bitterness of misery into which we with our clinging affections can enter with special comprehension, and which in our measure we may ourselves have known in stern reality.

If in our life's journey we have experienced the cruel piercing of our hand by the support on which we leant in fondest confidence, if change and forgetfulness have passed on the love or the friendship that was dearest to us on earth, if our hearts have been wrung by faithlessness where most we trusted, by desertion where we would have clung most strongly, if now we are alone and desolate who could once have said with joy to those we cherished most, "Ye are my friends,"—then let us rejoice, for in no other way could we have won so fully the sympathy of Him Who more than any that ever walked this earth has loved, and more than any other that ever lived has been forsaken,—"*and it was night.*"

Good Friday.

GOOD indeed! though on this supreme day there hangs the shadow of the great darkness which shrouded from all human eyes the death of the Creator; good with the eternal blessing of a world's salvation. What would have been the destiny of our unhappy race if this day had never dawned to make our fallen earth the altar of an all-sufficient Sacrifice? This incomplete, unsatisfactory life, with its delusive joys and bitter pains, must then have been our only hope, and death but an abyss of unfathomable gloom, ready to engulf us and those we love in the depths of some unknown despair. Good, then, indeed the day of suffering supreme, from whence sprang everlasting joy, the day when death became a Sacrament of Life Eternal.

E

To us who dare still in the Shadow of the Passion to follow CHRIST as He is taken from prison and from judgment, there seems no interval between this day and that which saw the dust of sad Gethsemane wet with the anguish-dew which sin in its utmost penalty wrung from the only One Who never yielded to its power, for each hour of that dreadful night is marked with its own special pain, and could we be content to rest in oblivion of it all, when for us it was endured? even if slumber overtake us through the weakness of the flesh, it is a night when we may say with truth, "*I sleep, but my heart waketh,*" for it cannot be that any one of its mournful watches should find us forgetting Him, Who doubtless in these commemorative hours, looks on us so often faithless, as once He looked on Peter and melted his very soul in anguish of repentance.

Slowly at length that memorable dawn appears, but how can we bear to contemplate the cruel hour that follows when "*by His stripes we are healed,*" when we "*beheld Him stricken, smitten of God and afflicted, wounded for our transgressions, bruised for our iniquities, and the chastisement of our peace is upon Him ?*"

Dearly purchased peace ! last legacy of our one Friend. To that peace may we cling though all the world should seek to rend it from us. May that peace be ours when the fair scenes of earth shall flash away for ever from our dying eyes, and through the far reaches of the deathless realms, may we pass on to Him Who is Himself our very and eternal Peace.

Not yet this day, however, must we lift up our heads in that dear hope, though our Redemption is drawing nigh, for still in the intense commemoration of the Holy Week the LORD is being led as a Lamb to the slaughter that He might pour out His soul unto death as an offering for sin, and so make intercession for the transgressors.

We may indeed dwell in thought with adoring gratitude on the many forms of suffering which bowed that Kingly Head beneath the crown of thorns, while He yielded Himself through the long bitter hours to the malice of the torturers, but we may not analyze the terrible details. Too often has the Sacrifice, whose unfathomable depths no human soul can comprehend, been profaned by well-meant efforts to bring it within the limits of poor earthly language, but the reverence of utter silence alone befits us when treading now in His wearied, fainting steps in the last stage of His remembered Passion, we pass onward with Him whither He goes bearing His Cross.

"*Weep not for Me, weep for yourselves.*"

To us and to all the human race till time shall be no longer was that injunction given, for JESUS knew that the guilt of those who inflicted on Him the utmost pangs of physical suffering, was light indeed to that incurred by all who through their own unholiness should crucify Him to themselves afresh, and put Him to an open shame. His murderers did it ignorantly in unbelief, but how often in the full blaze of the Gospel light, and especially in these latter days, men have denied the LORD that bought them, while even those who call themselves by His name reject Him secretly for some idol that enslaves their fancy, saying, "*Not this Man, but Barabbas.*"

Well for us if this day we can so weep for ourselves in our regretted past, that in future we may never have cause to weep for Him, crucified anew by our own cruel hands.

" I, if I be lifted up, will draw all men unto Me."

The hour has come marked out in its inde-
structible significance from the eternity wherein
it was foredoomed, and in which it shall for
ever be remembered; and we are drawn, as He
said, to that uplifted Sacrifice, the pledge and
embodiment of love undying, never more surely
to abandon Him Who in that tremendous hour
offered Himself up through the eternal Spirit
without spot to GOD. The blackness of night
has fallen upon Him and us, who waiting on
Him in spiritual realization, have reached this
central hour in all the history of the universe.
Even nature veils her face in her high noontide
from the sight of GOD by man deserted, and a
Man by GOD forsaken in His last extremity.

*" My God, My God, why hast Thou forsaken
Me ?"*

That terrible cry, laden with the inconceivable
misery, which must have been ours through
ceaseless cycles of existence if the Incarnate
SON had never lived on earth and died to bring
us back to the Bosom of the FATHER, teaches
us in so far as even thus we can comprehend it,
what would have been the eternal desolation of

our deathless souls in final exile from their GOD.

So long as the ages of this world's probation still endure, the echo of that mysterious cry will ascend to the throne of Immaculate Justice, till the last redeemed spirit has been won from the desert where GOD is not, to behold Him in His glory, and to enter into the joy of his LORD.

The reverent darkness still broods over the shuddering earth, and we in spirit cast ourselves beneath the pierced Feet to fix our whole heart, and mind, and strength on Him Who hangs there bearing our sins in His own body on the tree. Yet not only in heart-wrung gratitude and love must we lie there, while through the portentous gloom His dying Voice is heard to breathe the ineffable words which tell how He prays for His executioners, how He thirsts for our salvation, how He sanctifies all pure human affections by His care for His holy mother. We too have a sacrifice to offer, a crucifixion to accomplish. Those three hours of His last sufferings, " *Who took away the hand-writing that was against us, and nailed it to His Cross,*" must be the concentration of that daily dying unto sin to which we were bound when

we put on CHRIST in the waters of baptism.
We have been face to face with all that is evil
in ourselves through the weeks of Lenten preparation for this hour, and now upon the Cross
of our Redeemer we are called to crucify utterly
and for ever the whole body of sin in whatso-
ever form it separates us from the sinless LORD;
all cherished idols, all earthly hopes and dreams
that hold us back from GOD, our very being,
in truth, must be there transfixed in resolute
self-surrender, till every thought, and word, and
feeling is brought into captivity to the obedience
of CHRIST.

The complete and final crucifixion of our will
nailed to the will of GOD with the pierced
Hands and Feet of JESUS, is the special claim
made upon the soul by this the last Passion
day, and it is the most terrible of all the warnings of the Holy Week. There can be no pain-
less crucifixion. It may be that our very hearts
must break in yielding up that which has been
too absorbing or too dear. Yet even then when
we are stretched as it were with CHRIST upon
the rack of pain there is for us a consolation of
most heavenly sweetness, if with all our longing
souls we too can say, " *Lord, remember me*

when Thou comest to Thy kingdom," for then may we, even we, hope to be with Him one day in Paradise.

"*Consummatum est,"—it is finished!* finished the suffering and grief of JESUS, finished the sacrifice to omnipotent Justice, finished the world's salvation.

The portentous darkness is slowly lifted from the earth, and the pallid twilight shows the Divine One silent and still in death. JESUS is taken down from that now powerless Cross of pain and laid within His quiet grave, and already the peace which He bequeathed to us as His dying gift falls on our fainting souls, a peace pure and passionless, such as those alone can know whose natural self, slain by their own deliberate purpose, lies dead and buried in the Redeemer's tomb.

Easter Eve.

DIVINE unearthly day! dim indeed with the shadow of the valley of death, but instinct with a marvellous significance which draws our spirits into a strange consciousness of the realms of the departed.

"This day shalt thou be with Me in Paradise."

It almost seems to us on this day of heavenly rest, typical of the intermediate state, as if the words spoken to the penitent malefactor and fraught to him indeed with eternal blessedness, might yet in a limited sense be true of all who have sought to follow their beloved Master closely through the stages of His sacred Passion. For now dead with Him to all earthly desire, seeking JESUS alone in time and in eternity, we seem to rise from beneath His Cross where we too have offered up ourselves, and follow Him in spirit along the trackless way to the restful abodes of Hades. Turning from all human sights and sounds, we yield ourselves to the mysterious perception of the unseen state, which seems to be the peculiar grace accorded to those who keep this day in union with their departed LORD.

A supernatural stillness appears to be all around us with a cool soft air, such as breathes amid summer heat from some dark cavern deep among the rocks, while our whole spiritual intelligence thrills with intense realization of the Presence of our Incarnate GOD in the home of the faithful dead. We seem in some strange sense conscious that He is there, pervading the whole dim quiet atmosphere ; His Hands extended even as on the Cross in universal benediction, while at His Feet are resting calm and still the vast multitudes of our brethren gone before, drawn by His coming through the solemn shades to gather at that one Centre of all hope and joy. There amid the unnumbered throngs we seem to gain a veiled glimpse of beloved faces, vanished long since in mournful days from our longing eyes, and now, seeking for us no more, intent on Him alone for Whom they wait, their Resurrection and their Life.

With Him, with them, and all who have departed in His faith and fear, we may indeed abide this one calm day in Paradise, but since not yet for us the tyranny of life is overpast, it may not all be spent in peaceful contemplation of the rest that remains for the people of GOD.

We have yet a task to finish upon earth, we have to labour that we may indeed enter into that rest, lest in our bitter struggle with the enemies of GOD within us and without, we should after all come short of it. There is laid on us yet the stern necessity of becoming, in life, that which in death we would desire to be, for it seems plain that no new regeneration takes place within the undying soul when the mortal body is given to the dust; that which it has been in tendencies and desire upon earth, it still must be, when it goes out into the unknown realm where its eternal destiny shall be accomplished.

The lessons of the Holy Week which have taught us how to live, are now gathered up and concentrated in the teaching of this sacred Eve which instructs us how to die, not in words, but by the stupendous facts commemorated in it, which convey to us the certainty of those divine Truths, that have taken the sting from death, and robbed the grave of its victory. That grave need have no terrors for us now, since the Incarnate Love Himself has slept within its narrow walls, that He might render all the conditions of our nature pure and harmless in death as well as in life ; and this mysterious day should be the seal set on our immutable purpose, so to live in Him and with Him here, that we may pass through the grave and gate of death to be with Him for ever. The end of our years on earth may seem to us yet far off, and till it come, the troubled anxious interval is like that night of toil and sorrow, spent by the disciples on the stormy Tiberian sea, before the glorious dawn which brought them at last the blissful sight of their own Risen LORD.

We too are out upon the restless waves of life's dark sea, struggling with the baffling winds of error, and temptation, and toiling to reach the land of everlasting joy, and ever as we hurry onwards, the world grows drearier, and our spirits fainter, in their loneliness and gloom,— the scenes of youth and riper years recede into the distance, and the voices we have loved, die away from us to be heard no more, the lights of earth go out one by one, and the whelming waters rise higher and higher, as we drift we know not whither, helpless and alone.

The night—the dark unknown night whose mystery no living eye has ever pierced, is closing round us, yet we need not shrink or fear, for all will be well eternally, if only it can be said of each one of us, that when the morn was come—

" JESUS STOOD UPON THE SHORE."

DEVOTIONAL BOOKS.

THE DIVINE MASTER: a Devotional Manual illustrating the Way of the Cross. With Ten steel Engravings. Ninth Edition. Cloth, 2s. 6d.; morocco, 5s. Cheap Edition, in wrapper, 1s.

BENEATH THE CROSS. Readings for Children on our LORD's Seven Sayings. By FLORENCE WILFORD. Edited by CHARLOTTE M. YONGE. 18mo., cloth boards, 1s. 6d.; limp cloth, 1s.

THE LOVE OF THE ATONEMENT, a Devotional Exposition of the Fifty-third chapter of Isaiah. By the late Right Rev. R. MILMAN, D.D., Bishop of Calcutta. Fifth Edition. Fcap. 8vo., cloth, 3s. 6d.

MEDITATIONS ON THE SUFFERING LIFE OF OUR LORD. Translated from Pinart. Adapted to the use of the Anglican Church by A. P. FORBES, D.C.L., late Bishop of Brechin. Fifth Edition. Fcap. 8vo., cloth, 5s.

NOURISHMENT OF THE CHRISTIAN SOUL. Translated from Pinart. Adapted to the use of the Anglican Church by A. P. FORBES, D.C.L., late Bishop of Brechin. Fourth Edition. Fcap. 8vo., cloth, 5s.

THE MIRROR OF YOUNG CHRISTIANS. Translated from the French. Edited by A. P. FORBES, D.C.L., late Bishop of Brechin. With Engravings, 2s. 6d.

THE SEVEN WORDS FROM THE CROSS. A Devotional Commentary. By BELLARMINE. Second Edition. 1s. 6d.

MEDITATIONS ON THE MOST PRECIOUS BLOOD AND EXAMPLE OF CHRIST. By the Rev. J. S. TUTE, M.A., Vicar of Markington, Yorkshire. Fcap. 8vo., cl., 1s.

THE HIDDEN LIFE. Translated from Nepveu's Pensées Chrétiennes. Fourth Edition, enlarged. 18mo., 2s.

TWELVE SHORT AND SIMPLE MEDITATIONS ON THE SUFFERINGS OF OUR LORD JESUS CHRIST. Edited by the Rev. CANON BUTLER. 2s. 6d.

COMPANION FOR LENT. Being an Exhortation to Repentance, from the Syriac of S. Ephraem; and Thoughts for Every Day in Lent, gathered from other Eastern Fathers and Divines. By the Rev. S. C. MALAN, M.A. 1s. 3d.

THE CHRISTIAN'S DAY. By the Rev. F. E. PAGET, M.A. Royal 32mo., 2s. cloth.

London: J. MASTERS & Co., 78, New Bond Street.

www.ingramcontent.com/pod-product-compliance
Lightning Source LLC
Chambersburg PA
CBHW022030080426
42733CB00007B/787